Modelling with rigid bodies

Unit guide

The School Mathematics Project

CAMBRIDGE
UNIVERSITY PRESS

Main authors	Janet Jagger
	Ann Kitchen
	Tom Roper
Team leader	Ann Kitchen
Project director	Stan Dolan

The authors would like to give special thanks to Ann White for her help in preparing this book for publication.

Published by the Press Syndicate of the University of Cambridge
The Pitt Building, Trumpington Street, Cambridge CB2 1RP
40 West 20th Street, New York, NY 10011-4211, USA
10 Stamford Road, Oakleigh, Victoria 3166, Australia

First published 1993

Produced by 16-19 Mathematics and Laserwords, Southampton

Printed in Great Britain by Scotprint Ltd., Musselburgh.

ISBN 0 521 42654 5

Contents

Introduction to the unit
(for the teacher)

Modelling with rigid bodies is designed to follow *Modelling with circular motion*. It is independent of the work done in *Modelling with differential equations*. It is recognised that many students working through this text may be doing so without the benefit of substantial contact time with a teacher. The unit has therefore been written to facilitate 'supported self-study'. It is assumed that even a minimal allocation of teacher time will allow contact at the start and end of each chapter and so

- solutions to all thinking points and exercises are in the students' text;

- discussion points have been kept to a minimum;

- a special tutorial sheet can be used to focus discussion at a final tutorial on the work of the chapter.

Ideas for possible themes for an extended investigation are suggested throughout the unit. Students should be encouraged to respond to some of these challenges or to find others of their own choice, subject to teacher approval.

Chapter 1

The ideas about rigid body statics first met in *Modelling with force and motion* are extended here to introduce couples and the line of action of a resultant force. The content of tasksheet 3 may prove a fruitful source of extended investigations.

Chapter 2

Students can have difficulty with ideas on toppling and sliding. The practical work should enable them to identify any misconceptions they have. The theory used in calculating the position of the centre of gravity of a body may prove difficult and the discussion point will provide an opportunity for the teacher to help the student to overcome any problems.

Chapter 3

The tasksheets involve practical work which can easily be done by a student working alone. They should not be skimped. The work done in the tasksheet *Finding moments of inertia* could lead to a good investigation on moments of inertia of human bodies when engaged in various sports and the effects on the athletes.

Chapter 4

Angular acceleration of a body rotating around a fixed axis is dealt with in this chapter. Following its use in *Modelling with circular motion,* the dot notation for differentiation is used. The tasksheet about windscreen wipers should not be omitted. The activity makes the student think about suitable assumptions for modelling motion.

Chapter 5

The book finishes with the theory behind finding the force at the pivot of a rotating body. This theory is at the heart of many of the investigations that students may want to try. The chapter finishes with many real contexts that can be studied using the mechanics in the unit.

Throughout the unit, g should be assumed to be 10 ms^{-2} unless otherwise stated.

Tasksheets

1 Forces and couples

1.2 Normal contact forces and rigid bodies

> **A workman wants to slide a filing cabinet across the floor.**
>
> **(a)**   **Should he push it or pull it?**
>
> **(b)**   **What might happen when he tries to move it?**
>
> **(c)**   **Will it matter if the cabinet drawers are empty or full?**
>
> **(d)**   **If only one drawer is full, which one should it be to ensure the greatest stability?**

(a)   He should push it. There is a danger of the cabinet toppling over and he would not want it to fall on him.

(b)   It might stay where it is, in static equilibrium, it might slide, or it might start to rotate about the opposite edge.

(c)   The lighter the cabinet, the easier it will be to move it. This is because the limiting friction force depends on the normal contact force.

(d)   It will not affect the ease with which he can slide it across the floor but it will have an effect on whether the cabinet topples before it starts to slide. The lower down the drawer is, the more stable the cabinet will be, so the bottom drawer should be filled first. However, for safety you should **always** empty the drawers of a filing cabinet (and preferably remove the drawers themselves) before trying to move the cabinet.

Couples

1.   The effect will be an anticlockwise rotation of the lamina.

2.   The experiment should confirm the prediction.

3.   The moment about A is $6 \times 4 = 24$ Nm clockwise.

   The moment about D is $6 \times 4 = 24$ Nm clockwise.

   The moment about N is $6 \times 4 = 24$ Nm clockwise.

   The moment about M is $6 \times 2 + 6 \times 2 = 24$ Nm clockwise.

   The moment about P is $6 \times 2 + 6 \times 2 = 24$ Nm clockwise.

   The moment about Q is $6 \times 7 - 6 \times 3 = 24$ Nm clockwise.

   The moment about R is $6 \times 6 - 6 \times 2 = 24$ Nm clockwise.

   The moment appears to be independent of the point chosen.

4.   The moment about O is:

$$P \times AO - P \times BO = P(AO - BO)$$
$$= P \times AB$$
$$= Pd$$

This constitutes a partial proof of the conjecture made in the answer to question 3. The moment about O is independent of the position of O.

(For a complete proof, the case when O lies between the lines of action of the two forces P should also be considered.)

Forces about a pivot

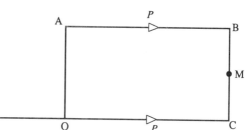

Case (i) Case (ii)

1.   In each case, the resultant force is P, parallel to AB.

2.   (a)   (i)   The moment about O is $P \times OA = Pd$, clockwise.
            (ii)   The moment about O is $P \times OA + P \times 0 + P \times 0 = Pd$, clockwise.

      (b)   (i)   The moment about A is $P \times 0 = 0$.
            (ii)   The moment about A is $P \times 0 + P \times AO - P \times AO = 0$.

      (c)   (i)   The moment about M is $P \times BM = \frac{1}{2}Pd$.
            (ii)   The moment about M is $P \times BM - P \times MC + P \times MC = \frac{1}{2}Pd$.

      (d)   (i)   (ii)

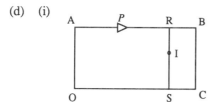

Moment = $P \times$ RI   Moment = $P \times$ RI $- P \times$ SI $+ P \times$ SI
                                              $= P \times$ RI

      (e)   (i)

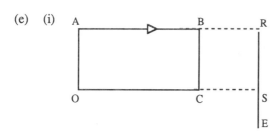

Moment = $P \times$ RE

(continued)

11

(ii)   Moment = P x RE $-$ P x SE $+$ P x SE
          = P x RE

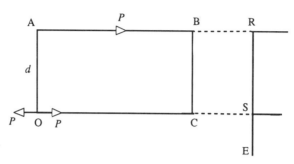

3.   Yes, they are equivalent.

4.   (a)   The resultant force has magnitude P parallel to AO.
                The couple = P x OC anticlockwise.

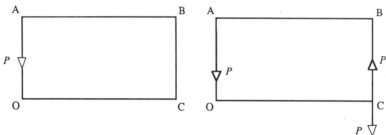

         (b)   The resultant force has magnitude P parallel to AB.
                The couple = P x $\frac{1}{2}BC$, anticlockwise

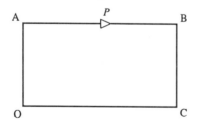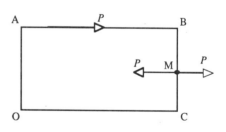

         (c)   The resultant force has magnitude $\sqrt{2}P$ at 45° to AB below AB.
                The couple = P(AB$-$AO), anticlockwise.

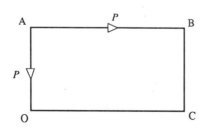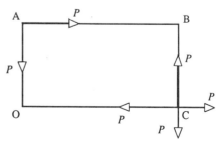

Moving bridges

1. **Set up a model**

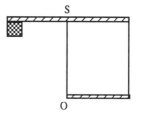

Model the counterweight as a particle of weight P newtons and the roadway as a rod of weight W newtons acting a distance $\frac{1}{2}a$ metres from the pivot.

Assume that the weight of the balance beam acts vertically down through O and therefore has no moment about O. Assume that the pivot at S is friction-free and that the contact force at the pivot is R newtons. Assume that the tension in each of the chains is $\frac{1}{2}T$, giving a total tension of T newtons.

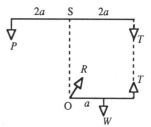

2. **Analyse the problem**

If the bridge is in equilibrium in any position, taking moments about O for the roadway:

$$T \times 2a \cos\theta = Wa \cos\theta$$
$$\Rightarrow \qquad T = \tfrac{1}{2}W$$

Taking moments about S for the balance beam:

$$P \times 2a \cos\theta = T \times 2a \cos\theta$$
$$\Rightarrow \qquad P = T, \quad \text{so } P = \tfrac{1}{2}W$$

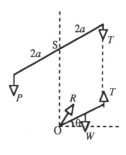

3. **Interpret**

If the counterweight is half the weight of the roadway then the bridge will stay open in any position. So a small extra downward force on the counterweight will make the bridge open and a small extra upward force will make it close.

4. If there is a retarding couple due to friction at the pivot then any force will have to overcome this before the bridge will move.
If the counterweight is large then its centre of mass may not be directly at the end of the beam. This means that the equation:

$$P \times 2a \cos\theta = T \times 2a \cos\theta$$

would not be true for all θ.

The further study of these bridges might make an interesting project.

1.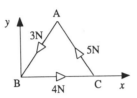

Taking axes as shown, if the resultant force is $\mathbf{R} = \begin{bmatrix} R_x \\ R_y \end{bmatrix}$,

resolving $R_x = 4 - 3\cos 60° - 5\cos 60° = 0$

$R_y = -3\sin 30° + 5\sin 30°$

$= \dfrac{2\sqrt{3}}{2} = \sqrt{3}$

Hence $\mathbf{R} = \begin{bmatrix} 0 \\ \sqrt{3} \end{bmatrix}$, a force of magnitude $\sqrt{3}$ newtons

whose line of action is perpendicular to BC.
Let it cut BC a distance x metres from B.

Taking moments about B,

$$5 \times \dfrac{\sqrt{3}}{2} = \sqrt{3}x$$

$$x = 2.5$$

2.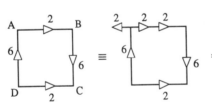

a force of magnitude 4 newtons along AB together with a couple of magnitude 8 Nm clockwise

OR resolving, $\mathbf{R} = \begin{bmatrix} 2+2 \\ 6-6 \end{bmatrix} = \begin{bmatrix} 4 \\ 0 \end{bmatrix}$

Taking moments about A, the couple is $6 \times 2 - 2 \times 2 = 8$ Nm clockwise.

3. If the pulley does not rotate, let the frictional couple be C Nm anticlockwise.

$$C + 10 \times 0.1 - 5 \times 0.1 = 0 \Rightarrow C = -0.5$$

The frictional couple is 0.5 Nm clockwise.

(continued)

4.

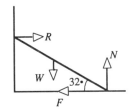

Take the forces as shown.
Using Newton's second law,

$$R - F = 0$$
$$N - W = 0$$

Since the ladder is about to slip, $F = \mu N$.

Taking moments about the foot of the ladder, taken to be of length $2a$,

$$Wa \cos 32° = R \times 2a \sin 32°$$

Substituting for W and R,

$$Na \cos 32° = \mu N \times 2a \sin 32°$$
$$\mu = \frac{\cos 32°}{2 \sin 32°} = 0.8$$

5.

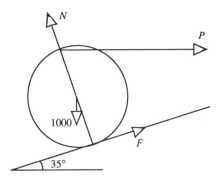

The reel is about to slip downwards.
Using Newton's second law along and perpendicular to the slope:

$$F + P \cos 35° - 1000 \sin 35° = 0 \quad ①$$
$$N - P \sin 35° - 1000 \cos 35° = 0 \quad ②$$

Taking moments about the point of contact,

$$P \times 2r \cos 35° = 1000r \sin 35°$$
$$P \cos 35° = 500 \sin 35°$$

Substituting in ①,

$$F = 500 \sin 35° = 286.8$$

Also $\quad P = 500 \tan 35° = 350.1$

Substituting in ②,

$$N = 1000 \cos 35° + 350.1 \sin 35°$$
$$= 1020$$

As the reel is about to slip, $F = \mu N$, so

$$\mu = \frac{286.8}{1020}$$
$$= 0.281 \quad \text{(to 3 s.f.)}$$

2 Toppling or sliding?

2.2 Centres of mass and centres of gravity

> **Are the centres of gravity and mass always at the same position?**
>
> (a) Re-work the example above with two weights $m_1 g_1$ and $m_2 g_2$, where g_1 and g_2 are the gravitational forces per unit kilogram for the masses m_1 and m_2 respectively, and $g_1 \neq g_2$. (You may assume that the vectors g_1 and g_2 are still parallel.)
>
> (b) Can you imagine circumstances where $g_1 \neq g_2$?

No. You found in *Modelling with force and motion* that they need not coincide if the body is not in a constant gravitational field.

(a) Let the gravitational force per unit mass for the mass m_1 be g_1 and that for the mass m_2 be g_2. The resultant weight is $m_1 g_1 + m_2 g_2$.

Taking moments about O, $(m_1 g_1 + m_2 g_2)\, \bar{x} = m_1 g_1 x_1 + m_2 g_2 x_2$

$$\Rightarrow \qquad \bar{x} = \frac{m_1 g_1 x_1 + m_2 g_2 x_2}{m_1 g_1 + m_2 g_2}$$

In this case, the gravitational field is not constant and so the expression cannot be simplified any further.

(b) In space, the gravitational force of a nearby object may be greater than that of distant suns.

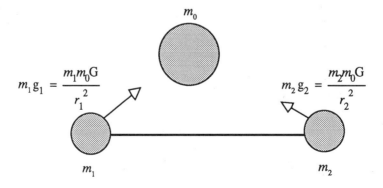

Toppling

1. The variables which might affect what happens are:

   • the height of the cylinder;
   • the radius of the cylinder;
   • the thickness of the cardboard;
   • the coefficient of friction between the slope and the cylinder.

2. You should be able to vary these one at a time to find the effect on the angle of slope at which the cylinder moves.

3. If the cylinder cannot slide then it will topple if $\tan \theta \geq \frac{2r}{h}$.

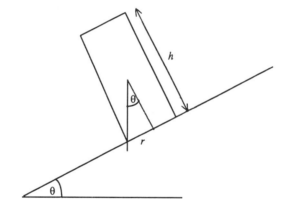

If the cylinder cannot topple, then it slides when $mg \sin \theta > \mu mg \cos \theta$, where μ is the coefficient of friction between the slope and the cylinder.

Thus it will slide when $\tan \theta > \mu$.

Whether the cylinder topples or slides depends upon which state is reached first as θ increases.

It topples first if $\tan \theta$ reaches $\frac{2r}{h}$ before it reaches μ.

It slides first if $\tan \theta$ reaches μ before it reaches $\frac{2r}{h}$.

Tutorial sheet

1.

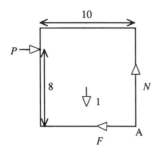

Let the friction force be F newtons and the normal contact force be N newtons.
The cube is about to topple when N acts through the edge of the cube as shown.

Taking moments about A,

$$0.08P = 1 \times 0.05$$
$$\Rightarrow \quad P = 0.625$$

So the cube will start to topple if P reaches 0.625.

It will slide if $F = \mu N$ and by Newton's second law, $P - F > 0$ and $N - 1 = 0$.

So $P > \mu N$, where $N = 1$ and $\mu = 0.4$.
The cube slides when $P > 0.4$.
It will slide before it topples.

2.

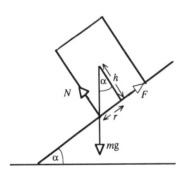

The cylinder will topple if the line of action of the weight is outside the base, that is if:

$$\tan \alpha > \frac{r}{h}$$

It will start to slide if $F = \mu N$ and by Newton's second law,

$$mg \sin \alpha - F > 0$$
and $$N - mg \cos \alpha = 0$$
so it slides if $$mg \sin \alpha > \mu mg \cos \alpha$$
$$\tan \alpha > \mu$$

It will slide before it topples if $\mu \le \frac{r}{h}$.

3.

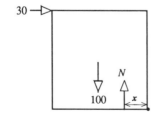

The packing case will topple when the line of action of N is clear of the lorry.
By Newton's second law, $N - 100 = 0$
Taking moments about the edge of the case,

$$100 \times 0.75 - 30 \times 1.5 - 100x = 0$$
$$\Rightarrow \quad x = 0.3$$

The case is about to fall when 0.3 metre overhangs the edge.

(continued)

4.   If the heights of two similar **hollow** cones are in the ratio 1 : 3 their masses are in the ratio 1 : 9. (**Solid** cones would have their masses in the ratio 1 : 27.)

So if the complete cone has mass $9M$, the small cone has mass M and the remainder has mass $8M$.

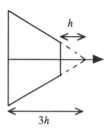

Let the centre of mass of the remainder be a distance d metres from the base. Then,

$$8M \times d + M \times \left(2h + \frac{h}{3}\right) = 9M \times \left(\frac{3h}{3}\right)$$

$$\Rightarrow \qquad 8d = 9h - \frac{7h}{3}$$

$$d = \frac{20h}{24} = \frac{5h}{6}$$

5.

Let the centre of mass be at the point $(\bar{x}, 0)$.
Let the density be ρ kg m^{-3}.
Mass of large cylinder $= \rho\pi h(R + d)^2 - \rho\pi hR^2$
Mass of small cylinder $= \rho\pi h(r + d)^2 - \rho\pi hr^2$

Taking moments about the y-axis,

$$\bar{x}\rho\pi h(2Rd + d^2 + 2rd + d^2) = \frac{h}{2}\rho\pi h(2Rd + d^2) + \frac{3h}{2}\rho\pi h(2rd + d^2)$$

$$\bar{x}[2d(R + r + d)] = \frac{h}{2}(2Rd + d^2 + 6rd + 3d^2)$$

$$= h(Rd + 3rd + 2d^2)$$

$$\bar{x} = \frac{h(R + 3r + 2d)}{2(R + r + d)}$$

3 *Rotation and energy*

3.1 Rotational energy

> **Find the kinetic energy of the rotating rod, modelling it as a set of small particles.**

Consider a particle P of mass m kilograms a distance r metres from the centre.

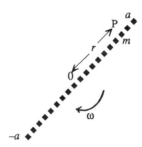

It is moving with speed $v = r\omega$ m s^{-1} at a right angle to the rod.

Its kinetic energy is $\frac{1}{2}mv^2$

$$= \frac{1}{2}m\,(r\omega)^2 \text{ joules}$$

Every particle is moving with the same angular speed ω, so the total KE is:

$$\sum_{-a}^{a} \frac{1}{2}mr^2\omega^2 = \frac{1}{2}\left(\sum mr^2\right)\omega^2 \text{ joules}$$

So, even though the centre of mass of the rod is not moving, the rod has kinetic energy due to its rotation. This is called rotational kinetic energy and is measured in kg m^2 s^{-2} or joules (the same units as those used for linear kinetic energy).

Rotating bodies

1. The rod should be easy to start spinning. Your finger applied a force to the rod and the point of application was moving in the direction of rotation. Your finger was therefore doing work.

2. You should find that you have to use a little more force this time or apply the same force for a longer time. You therefore do more work.

3. As you move the Blu-Tack outwards the work needed increases.

4. For a given mass, the work needed varies according to the way in which that mass is distributed. The tasksheet intends you to apply Blu-Tack symmetrically but interesting further discussion arises when asymmetrical distributions are considered.

6. (a) The complete rod has zero linear momentum.

   (b) The rotational motion results in rotational momentum and energy.

   (c) Work was done to set it spinning so that it should have kinetic energy.

7. The particle model is not appropriate for this situation. Assuming that Blu-Tack is applied symmetrically the particle would be at the pivot point and would have no kinetic energy.

Finding moments of inertia

1.   –

2.   –

3.   You should find that the length of the string (measured to the middle of the piece of Blu-Tack) should be about two-thirds of the length of the rod. This will vary slightly if the hole is not right at the end of the rod. If l is the length of the string and d is the length of the rod, then $l = \frac{2}{3}d$.

4.   The angular speeds of the string and the rod should be equal at all times.

5.   String

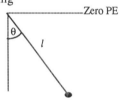

Initial PE $= -mgl \cos \theta$ Initial KE $= 0$

Final PE $= -mgl$ Final KE $= 0.5m(l\omega)^2$

Energy equation:
$$-mgl \cos \theta = -mgl + 0.5l^2\omega^2$$
$$\Rightarrow \quad mgl\,(1 - \cos \theta) = 0.5l^2\omega^2 \qquad ①$$

Rod

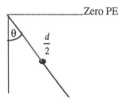

Initial PE $= -mg\frac{d}{2}\cos \theta$ Initial KE $= 0$

Final PE $= -mg\frac{d}{2}$ Final KE $= 0.5I\omega^2$

Using the same method:

$$mg\,\frac{d}{2}\,(1 - \cos \theta) = 0.5I\omega^2 \qquad ②$$

From ① $\omega^2 = \dfrac{2g\,(1-\cos\theta)}{l}$.   Substituting in ②, $mg\,\dfrac{d}{2}(1 - \cos \theta) = \dfrac{Ig\,(1-\cos\theta)}{l}$

But $1 - \cos \theta \neq 0$ so $I = \frac{1}{2}mld$

7.   If $l = \frac{2}{3}d$ then $I = \frac{1}{3}md^2$ which is the moment of inertia about one end of a rod of length d.

8.   Remember to measure $\frac{d}{2}$ from the pivot point to the centre of gravity of your gymnast.

1. Moment of inertia of the rod about centre $= \frac{1}{3} ma^2 = \frac{1}{3} \times 0.3 \times 0.1^2$

$$= 0.001 \text{ kg m}^2$$

Moment of inertia of the rod about point 5 cm from centre $= 0.001 + 0.3 \times 0.05^2$

$$= 0.001 \, 75 \text{ kg m}^2$$

$KE = \frac{1}{2} I \omega^2$

$\quad = \frac{1}{2} \times 0.00175 \times 20^2 = 0.35 \text{ joule}$

2. (a) Moment of inertia of AB about A is $\frac{4}{3} \times 200 \times 6^2 = 9600 \text{ kg m}^2$

Moment of inertia of CD about A is $\frac{1}{3} \times 600 \times 6^2 + 600 \times 12^2 = 93\,600 \text{ kg m}^2$

Total moment of inertia $= 103\,200 \text{ kg m}^2$

(b)

Initial PE $= -200 \times 10 \times 6 - 600 \times 10 \times 12$

$$= -84\,000 \text{ joules}$$

Initial KE $= \frac{1}{2} I \omega^2 = \frac{103\,200}{2} \times 0.5^2$

$$= 12\,900 \text{ joules}$$

Final PE $= -200 \times 10 \times 6 \cos \theta - 600 \times 10 \times 12 \cos \theta = -84\,000 \cos \theta$ joules

Final KE $= 0$

Ignoring any energy loss, $-84\,000 \cos \theta = 12\,900 - 84\,000$

$\Rightarrow \quad \cos \theta = 0.846$

So the maximum height of B is $12\,(1 - \cos \theta) = 1.84$ metres.

(continued)

(c) Modelling the boat as a particle of mass 800 kg at B and taking the horizontal through B as the zero PE line:

Initial KE $= \frac{1}{2} mv^2 = \frac{1}{2} \times 800 \times (12 \times 0.5)^2 = 14\,400$ joules

Initial PE $= 0$

Final KE $= 0$

Final PE $= 800 \times 10 \times h$, where h metres is the height reached. Assuming that energy is conserved,

$$8000h = 14\,400 \Rightarrow h = 1.8$$

Using this model, the maximum height of B is 1.8 metres, slightly less than that obtained in part (b).

3.   (a) If the chimney is modelled as a rod of length 20 metres:

Moment of inertia about AB is $\frac{4}{3} \times 3000 \times 100 = 400\,000$ kg m^2

Assuming conservation of energy, $3000 \times 10 \times 10 = \frac{1}{2} \times 400\,000 \times \omega^2$

$$\omega^2 = \frac{3}{2} \Rightarrow \omega = 1.22 \text{ rad s}^{-1}$$

The speed is $20\omega = 24.5$ ms^{-1}

(b) If the chimney is modelled as a rectangular lamina 20 metres by 2 metres:

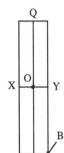

Moment of inertia of the lamina about XY $= \frac{1}{3} \times 3000 \times 10^2$

$$= 100\,000 \text{ kg m}^2$$

Moment of inertia about QP $= \frac{1}{3} \times 3000 \times 1^2 = 1000$ kg m^2

Moment of inertia of the lamina about axis through 0, the centre of mass, perpendicular to the lamina $= 101\,000$ kg m^2 (by the perpendicular axes theorem)

Moment of inertia of the lamina about AB $= 101\,000 + 3000 \times (10^2 + 1^2)$
$$= 404\,000 \text{ kg m}^2$$

Assuming conservation of energy, if the angular speed when the chimney hits the ground is ω,

$$3000g \times 9 = \frac{1}{2}(404\,000)\,\omega^2$$
$$\Rightarrow \omega = 1.16 \text{ rad s}^{-1}$$

The speed of the top of the chimney is 23.1 ms^{-1}.

The speed is very little different from that obtained in part (a). The simple model seems a reasonable one.

4 Rotation and angular acceleration

4.1   Moment of momentum – angular momentum

> **A potter drops a large lump of clay onto the centre of a freely spinning potter's wheel. What do you think happens to the angular speed of the wheel?**
>
> **Does your answer depend on:**
>
> **(a)   the mass of the clay;**
>
> **(b)   the shape of the clay?**

The clay will start to spin round at the same speed as the wheel. If the wheel does not change speed as the clay lands then the angular momentum of the system would be increased. This suggests that the angular speed of the wheel must decrease to compensate for the increase in angular speed of the clay, while total angular momentum remains constant.

(a)   A heavy lump of clay affects the speed more than a lighter lump. Consider, for example, two lumps of clay each in the form of cylinders having the same radius. If the height (and mass) of one is twice that of the other then so is the moment of inertia about the axis.

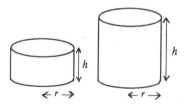

For a given change in momentum, the change in angular speed of the larger lump would be only half that for the smaller lump.

(b)   A lump at the centre of the wheel affects the speed of the wheel less than a lump of similar mass but spread out over the wheel.

Continuing to use the model of a cylinder of radius r, as r increases then the moment of inertia increases and hence the angular momentum for a given angular speed increases. Hence, the greater is r, the smaller the final angular speed of the wheel and clay.

The windscreen wiper

1.   (a)   The blade on one make of car were found to be 50 cm long. They completed an oscillation in 1 second (on 'fast wipe'). The angle traced out was $150° = \frac{5}{6}\pi$ radians. Your measurements may differ somewhat from these but the remaining commentary will be based upon these figures.

The length of the path of the tip is $\frac{5\pi}{6} \times 0.5$ metres each way.

So the speed of the tip is 2.6 ms^{-1}.

(b)   The angular speed, $\omega = \frac{5\pi}{3} = 5.24 \text{ rad s}^{-1}$

The acceleration is $\omega^2 r = 13.7 \text{ ms}^{-2}$ radially.

2.   The blades change direction at each end of the path, so the speed at A and B is zero. The speed-time graph might be as indicated below:

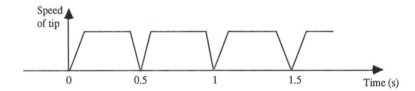

The second model attempts to obtain this type of graph for the speed.

3.   (a)   A complete oscillation takes 1 second and so $p = 2\pi$.

$\theta_{min} = 0 \implies b = -a.$

$\theta_{max} = \frac{5}{6}\pi \implies a = \frac{5}{12}\pi$

Hence $\theta = \frac{5}{12}\pi(1 - \cos 2\pi t)$

(b)   Then $\dot{\theta} = \frac{5}{6}\pi^2 \sin 2\pi t, \ \ddot{\theta} = \frac{5}{3}\pi^3 \cos 2\pi t.$

$v = 0.5\dot{\theta} = \frac{5}{12}\pi^2 \sin 2\pi t$

The accleration is $\frac{1}{2}\left(\frac{5}{6}\pi^2 \sin 2\pi t\right)^2 \approx 33.8 \sin^2 2\pi t$ radially

$\frac{1}{2}\left(\frac{5}{3}\pi^3 \cos 2\pi t\right) \approx 25.8 \cos 2\pi t$ tangentially

(continued)

4. Graphs of speed against time for both models are as shown:

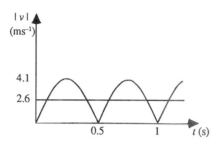

The second model has the advantage that it describes the changes of direction at the extreme points. In particular, it gives an estimate for the tangential acceleration of the tips of the wiper blades.

Flywheels

The purpose of this tasksheet is to explain why flywheels are important, as well as to provide practice in modelling.

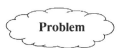 **Problem**   To find a relationship between the moment of inertia of a flywheel about its axis of rotation and the rate of change of angular velocity due to a given torque.

1.   **Set up a model**   Assume that the flywheel has moment of inertia I kg m² about the axis of rotation.

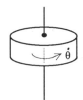

Assume that the torque is C Nm in the direction of rotation.

Assume that the rate of change of angular velocity is $\ddot{\theta}$ and that $\theta = \dot{\theta} = 0$ when $t = 0$.

Analyse   Rate of change of angular velocity $= \dfrac{d\dot{\theta}}{dt} = \ddot{\theta}$

$$I\ddot{\theta} = C \Rightarrow \ddot{\theta} = \frac{C}{I}$$

2.   **Interpret**   If C is positive, for example if it is due to a driving force, then the angular velocity increases.

If C is negative, for example if it is due to a friction force, the angular velocity decreases.

For a given torque, flywheels with greater moments of inertia have smaller rates of change of angular velocity than those with small moments of inertia.

1. Angular momentum $= I\dot{\theta} \Rightarrow 56 = 40\dot{\theta} \Rightarrow \dot{\theta} = 1.4$ rad s^{-1}

2. Initial angular momentum $= 1 \times 15$

    Moment of inertia of clay $= \dfrac{Mr^2}{2} = 0.01$ kg m^2

    There is no external torque so angular momentum is conserved.

    If ω is the new angular speed,
    $$15 = 1.01\,\omega \Rightarrow \omega = 14.9 \text{ rad s}^{-1}$$

3. (a) Let C be the resisting torque and $\ddot{\theta}$ the resulting angular deceleration.
    Then $C = I\ddot{\theta}$ and, since C and I are constant, $\ddot{\theta}$ is constant.

    So $\ddot{\theta} = \dfrac{0-6}{2} = -3$ rad s^{-1} and $C = 0.5 \times (-3) = -1.5$ newton metres

    (b) $\ddot{\theta} = -3 \Rightarrow \dot{\theta} = -3t + 6$ (since $\dot{\theta} = 6$ when $t = 0$)
    $$\Rightarrow \theta = -1.5t^2 + 6t \quad \text{(since } \theta = 0 \text{ when } t = 0\text{)}$$

    When $t = 2$, $\theta = 6$.

    Thus the wheel has rotated through 6 radians.

4. (a)
    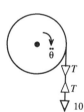

    The acceleration of the mass is $a\ddot{\theta}$.
    $$10 - T = 1 \times 0.15\ddot{\theta} \qquad\qquad ①$$
    The torque is $T \times 0.15$, so
    $$0.15\,T = 0.01\ddot{\theta} \qquad\qquad ②$$

    Eliminating T from ① and ②, $1.5 = (0.0225 + 0.01)\ddot{\theta} \Rightarrow \ddot{\theta} = 46.2$ rad s^{-2}
    The acceleration is 6.93 ms^{-2}

    (b) $\dot{\theta} = 46.2t + 0$ (as $\dot{\theta} = 0$ when $t = 0$)
    So when $t = 0.5$, $\dot{\theta} = 23.1$ rad s^{-1}

    (c) $\theta = 23.1t^2 + 0$ (as $\theta = 0$ when $t = 0$)
    The distance fallen is $0.15 \times \theta = 0.15 \times 23.1 \times (0.5)^2$
    $$= 0.87 \text{ metre}$$

5 Modelling with rigid bodies

5.1 The force at the pivot

(a) Write down the equation of rotational motion for the pirate ship.

(b) Write $I = \lambda M$ (where λ is a constant) and assume that the frictional couple is negligible. Then show that the component Y of the force at O is given by:

$$Y = Mg \left(1 - \frac{a^2}{\lambda}\right) \sin \theta$$

(a) The equation of rotational motion is $I\ddot{\theta} = -Mga \sin \theta - C$

(b) $\lambda M \ddot{\theta} = -Mga \sin \theta$ as $C = 0$

$$\Rightarrow \ddot{\theta} = \frac{-ga \sin \theta}{\lambda}$$

$X - Mg \cos \theta = Ma\, \dot{\theta}^2$

$Y - Mg \sin \theta = Ma\, \ddot{\theta}$

$$= \frac{-Maga \sin \theta}{\lambda}$$

$$\Rightarrow \qquad Y = Mg \sin \theta \left(1 - \frac{a^2}{\lambda}\right)$$

1.   (a)   Assume that the rod makes an angle of θ with the vertical.

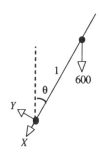

By Newton's second law,

$$X + 600 \cos \theta = 60 \times 1 \times \dot{\theta}^2 \qquad ①$$

$$600 \sin \theta - Y = 60 \times 1 \times \ddot{\theta} \qquad ②$$

Energy is conserved, so

$$600 (1 - 1 \cos \theta) = \frac{1}{2} \times 60 \times (1 \times \dot{\theta})^2$$

$$\dot{\theta}^2 = 20 - 20 \cos \theta$$

Then from ①, $X = 1200 - 1200 \cos \theta - 600 \cos \theta$

$$= 1200 - 1800 \cos \theta$$

When $\theta = 90°$, $X = 1200$ newtons and when $\theta = 180°$, $X = 3000$ newtons.

Using the equation of rotational motion,

$$60 \times 1^2 \times \ddot{\theta} = 600 \times 1 \sin \theta$$

$$\ddot{\theta} = 10 \sin \theta$$

Substituting this value in ②,

$$Y = 600 \sin \theta - 600 \sin \theta = 0$$

$$\Rightarrow \quad Y = 0$$

The force on her hands is always directed along the arms. It is 1200 newtons when she is horizontal and 3000 newtons when she is at the lowest point of the swing.

    (b)   Assume that the rod makes an angle θ with the vertical.

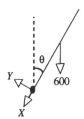

By Newton's second law, equations ① and ② again apply.

Energy is conserved:

$$600 (1 - 1 \cos \theta) = \frac{1}{2} \times I \times \dot{\theta}^2 = \frac{1}{2} \times \frac{4}{3} \times 60 \times 1^2 \times \dot{\theta}^2$$

$$\dot{\theta}^2 = 15 - 15 \cos \theta$$

From ① $X = 900 - 1500 \cos \theta$

(continued)

So $X = 900$ newtons when $\theta = 90°$ and 2400 newtons when $\theta = 180°$.

Using the equation of rotational motion,

$$\tfrac{4}{3} \times 60 \times 1^2 \times \ddot{\theta} = 600 \sin\theta \;\Rightarrow\; \ddot{\theta} = \tfrac{15}{2}\sin\theta$$

So equation ② becomes

$$600 \sin\theta - Y = 450 \sin\theta$$

$$Y = 150 \sin\theta$$

When $\theta = 90°$, $Y = 150$ newtons and when $\theta = 180°$, $Y = 0$

The force on her hands is $\sqrt{(900^2 + 150^2)} \approx 912$ newtons when she is horizontal and 2400 newtons at the lowest point of her swing.

2. (a)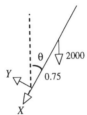

By Newton's second law,

$$X + 2000 \cos\theta = 200 \times 0.75\, \dot{\theta}^2 = 150\, \dot{\theta}^2 \quad ①$$

$$2000 \sin\theta - Y = 200 \times 0.75\, \ddot{\theta} = 150\, \ddot{\theta} \quad ②$$

Energy is conserved. So, since the tail-gate starts from rest,

$$2000\,(0.75 - 0.75 \cos\theta) = \tfrac{1}{2} \times \tfrac{4}{3} \times 200 \times 0.75^2 \times \dot{\theta}^2$$

$$1500 - 1500 \cos\theta = 75\, \dot{\theta}^2$$

Substituting in ①, $X = 3000 - 3000 \cos\theta - 2000 \cos\theta$

$$= 3000 - 5000 \cos\theta$$

Using the equation of rotational motion $I\ddot{\theta} = \sum Fr$,

$$150\, \ddot{\theta} = 2000 \times 0.75 \sin\theta$$

Substituting in ②, $Y = 2000 \sin\theta - 1500 \sin\theta = 500 \sin\theta$

The radial and tangential components of the force at the hinges are $3000 - 5000 \cos\theta$ and $500 \sin\theta$ newtons.

(b) When $\theta = 180°$, $1500 + 1500 = 75\, \dot{\theta}^2 \;\Rightarrow\; \dot{\theta} \approx 6.3$ rad s^{-1}

(c) When $\theta = 180°$, $X = 8000$ newtons and $Y = 0$.

The contact force is 8000 newtons in a vertical direction.